THE LITTLE BOOK OF

LIVERPOOL LEGENDS

Independent and Unofficial

First published in 2025 by OH
An Imprint of HEADLINE PUBLISHING GROUP LIMITED

1

Disclaimer:

Cataloguing in Publication Data is available from the British Library

ISBN 978-1-03542-284-5

Compiled and written by: David Clayton
Editorial: Chris Stone and Matt Tomlinson
Designed and typset in Helvetica Now by: Tony Seddon
Project manager: Russell Porter
Production: Marion Storz
Printed and bound in Dubai

MIX
Paper | Supporting
responsible forestry
FSC® C104740

Headline's policy is to use papers that are natural, renewable and recyclable products and made from wood grown in well-managed forests and other controlled sources. The logging and manufacturing processes are expected to conform to the environmental regulations of the country of origin.

HEADLINE PUBLISHING GROUP LIMITED
An Hachette UK Company
Carmelite House, 50 Victoria Embankment, London EC4Y 0DZ

The authorised representative in the EEA is Hachette Ireland, 8 Castlecourt Centre, Dublin 15, D15 XTP3, Ireland (email: info@hbgi.ie)

www.headline.co.uk   www.hachette.co.uk

THE LITTLE BOOK OF

LIVERPOOL LEGENDS

Independent and Unofficial

THE GREATEST PLAYERS TO WEAR THE SHIRT
AND THE GREATEST MANAGERS TO LEAD THE TEAM

CONTENTS

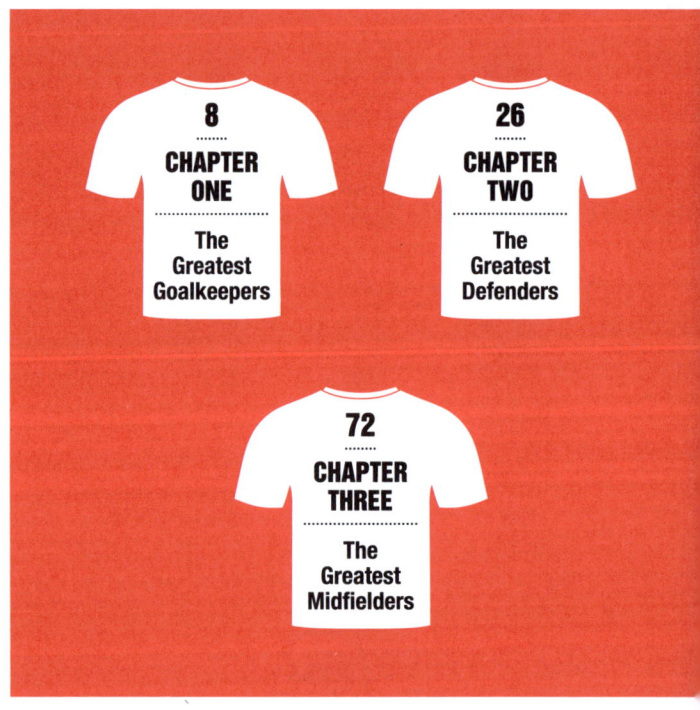

INTRODUCTION

Liverpool Football Club. Just those three words evoke a history that is both unique and cherished all over the world.

Liverpool are a truly global club with a fanbase to match, but what is it about this football club that makes it so special? Is it the supporters? Anfield? The Kop? Or could it be the generations of wonderful players and managers that have represented the Reds over the years?

It's impossible to think about Liverpool without thinking of Bill Shankly and Bob Paisley. Kevin Keegan, Kenny Dalglish, Ray Clemence... stellar names and legends all. But if they were all from a bygone era, Jürgen Klopp, Mo Salah and Virgil van Dijk are very much from more modern times.

Of course, the connection with The Beatles and the spine-tingling anthem "You'll Never Walk Alone", sang on a packed and swaying Kop, are equally synonymous with Liverpool FC. After all, Liverpool city itself is imbued with the same indefinable magic; a place that has contributed as much to the world as cities many times bigger. And these players and managers know better than anyone that if you give your all to Liverpool, Liverpool will give it all back. Once a Red, always a Red.

In the pages that follow, you'll discover the players and managers that have stood out and remained in the memories of those lucky enough to have seen them. These icons of the club embody the best of Liverpool, from the fearsome fighting spirit of Tommy Smith to the loyal longevity of Jamie Carragher.

From the past, to the here and now, *The Little Book of Liverpool Legends* showcases the giants that have made this football club what it is today.

CHAPTER

1

THE GREATEST GOALKEEPERS

That there are only four
goalkeepers in our opening chapter
is not down to a lack of quality –
more the longevity and excellence
of those included...

Ray Clemence
1967 – 1981

When both Bill Shankly and Bob Paisley keep you as their No. 1 throughout their time as manager, you must be doing something right!

As it happens, Ray Clemence was very, very good. He remains one of the greatest goalkeepers of modern times and certainly has to be in the mix to be considered as the club's best custodian of all-time. His battle for the England jersey with Peter Shilton went on throughout the seventies, with no England manager able to separate them. Reliable, with excellent handling, he was the perfect man to keep goal during Liverpool's glory years.

GAMES

League 470
FA Cup 54
League Cup 55
Europe 80
Other 6
Total **665**

TROPHIES

First Division x 5
FA Cup x 1
League Cup x 1
FA Charity Shield x 5

European Cup x 3
UEFA Cup x 2
European Super Cup x 1

He's a nicely built lad, with one or two mannerisms, and maybe a wee bit cocky. But we're getting him in plenty of time to work on him.

BILL SHANKLY

On the field he was a very natural goalkeeper. He was tall and incredibly athletic and had great hands. Ray was totally reliable and unfussy. He was not showy or extravagant but of his era there were very few better.

PETER SHILTON

I couldn't play anywhere else. I never wanted to be a goalkeeper. The sports master nominated me to go into goal. When I went into goal it was just natural for me to do.

RAY CLEMENCE

My mum had phoned the council to send someone to find me. She'd had a call from the club to say Scunthorpe had agreed a fee with Liverpool and it was up to me if I wanted to go. My life changed at that moment, as I'm standing there stacking deckchairs.

RAY CLEMENCE

on learning he was about to become a Liverpool player

Bruce Grobbelaar
1981 – 1994

Bruce Grobbelaar represented Liverpool between 1981 and 1994, becoming one of English football's most memorable characters in the process.

The Zimbabwean is best remembered for his eccentric playing style, which occasionally saw him performing handstands during games or even swinging from the crossbar.

For all his flamboyance and occasional clowning around, he was a very good goalkeeper, often cited as one of the original "sweeper keepers". After joining the Reds from Crewe, he went on to make 628 appearances and will be forever remembered for his famous "spaghetti legs" penalty shoot-out routine that helped Liverpool win the European Cup in 1984.

GAMES

League 440
FA Cup 62
League Cup 70
Europe 38
Other 18
Total **628**

TROPHIES

First Division x 6
FA Cup x 3
League Cup x 3
FA Charity Shield x 5

European Cup x 1

Brucie, Brucie, give us a wave.

THE KOP

and Brucie would never disappoint

Everybody has an opinion about Bruce Grobbelaar, but it's the opinion of the men who play in front of him that matters most. If they lost confidence in him, he wouldn't last five minutes. But Liverpool defenders have always had a greater appreciation of him than anybody else.

BOB PAISLEY

I had to learn some hard lessons in my early days because I was a bit of a showman, a kind of Jekyll and Hyde character.

BRUCE GROBBELAAR

on his early eccentricities at Anfield

When you go out on to that field it's going to be war. Sportsmanship is playing to the best of your abilities and then, afterwards, shaking your opponent's hand.

BRUCE GROBBELAAR

Pepe Reina
2005 – 2014

When Pepe Reina joined Liverpool in 2005, few could have realised the impact he would have with the club. He made his debut in the UEFA Super Cup and never looked back, keeping the No. 1 jersey for the next eight seasons and claiming the Premier League Golden Glove award in his first three seasons.

Another early prototype for the sweeper-keeper of today – when required, Reina was a leader from the back, dominating his area with his commanding presence. He was also an excellent shot-stopper, was good with the ball at his feet and a formidable presence when facing penalties – all in all, a top keeper who paid back his transfer fee many times over.

GAMES

League 285
FA Cup.................................... 14
League Cup 8
Europe.................................... 84
Other 3
Total 394

TROPHIES

FA Cup x 1
League Cup x 1
FA Community Shield x 1

UEFA Super Cup x 1

This consistency makes him a top-class goalkeeper. I would say he is one of the best keepers in the world now. When we signed him I said he was the best in Spain and Iker Casillas was doing really well too. Our fans know he's really important, and some journalists also. If they know about football, they can see the difference between Pepe and the other keepers.

RAFA BENITEZ

He is extremely quick, has great reflexes, is very brave and is a good kicker of the ball. If you put all those qualities together then you have a very good goalkeeper.

RAY CLEMENCE

My time in England is where I have felt
truly like a footballer, and I have put my
name among the best players. I'm very
proud to have played almost 400
games with Liverpool.

PEPE REINA

I consider Liverpool my home, and it will always
be like that. It's what they say: once a Red,
always a Red.

PEPE REINA

Alisson Becker

2018 – present day

Integral to one of the best Liverpool sides of modern times, Brazilian goalkeeper Alisson Becker has helped define the way modern goalkeepers play.

Equally comfortable saving shots as he is with the ball at his feet, his pinpoint distribution was a key component to Jürgen Klopp's high-octane Liverpool side that went toe-to-toe with Manchester City in numerous title races.

A calming influence and an excellent shot-stopper, Alisson has earned his place among the pantheon of legendary Liverpool goalkeepers and is also regarded as one of the world's greats.

GAMES*

League 215
FA Cup................................... 9
League Cup 2
Europe................................... 52
Other..................................... 4
Total............................ **282**

* as of 31/01/2025

TROPHIES

Premier League x 1
FA Cup x 1
League Cup x 1

Champions League x 1
FIFA Club World Cup x 1

Is Alisson worth €50m? Don't be silly, he's worth far more than that... I don't think many people have realised who Alisson is. This guy is a phenomenon. He is the Number One of Number Ones. He is the Messi of goalkeepers, because he has the same mentality as Messi. He is a goalkeeper who can mark an era.

ROBERTO NEGRISOLO

the former Roma goalkeeper coach lauds Alisson

Alisson is a surprise only for those who haven't seen him before. What really strikes me is how he deals with dangerous situations so efficiently. That gives his team a lot of confidence.

GIANLUIGI BUFFON

I like to focus on good positioning. If you have that, you are one step in front of the opponent. If you can act before having to react, it is better. I try to read the game as well, read the striker, look at his movements.

ALISSON BECKER

I'm too emotional these last months for everything that happened with me, with my family. Football is my life, I played since I remember as a human being with my father. I hope he was here to see it but I'm sure that he's seeing with God on his side and celebrating.

ALISSON BECKER

on his injury-time goal against West Brom in 2021

CHAPTER
2

THE GREATEST DEFENDERS

Liverpool have always prided themselves on having some truly great defenders. From classy ball-playing centre-halves to gnarly no-nonsense men of steel who were adored by the Kop...

Alan Hansen

1977 – 1991

Alan Hansen was a classy, easy-on-the-eye central defender that only the Reds seemed to produce at one time.

The graceful Scot had it all. Comfortable in every aspect of his play and an excellent distributor of the ball, he was also quick and commanding in the air.

He could tackle, too, and would enjoy nothing more than dispossessing a forward with his superb reading of the game then surging out of defence with the ball to start a counterattack. A quality act that, like a fine wine, seemed to get better with age.

GAMES and GOALS

League	434	8
FA Cup	58	2
League Cup	68	1
Europe	46	3
Other	14	0
Total	**620**	**14**

TROPHIES

First Division x 8

FA Cup x 2

League Cup x 4

FA Charity Shield x 6

European Cup x 3

UEFA Super Cup x 1

He has a very measured, long stride and is much faster than he looks. I can't think of more than a couple of players who could beat him over 100 metres. He has both the ability and the patience to launch attacks from deep positions.

BOB PAISLEY

Football was just so easy for Alan, too easy really. It never felt very fair.

MARK LAWRENSON

I always wanted to be a golfer, only I realised that
if I'd played golf I would have been skint.

ALAN HANSEN

A good defender is like a rock. Strong, unyielding,
and always in control.

ALAN HANSEN

Emlyn Hughes
1967 – 1979

Emlyn Hughes was a wonderful Liverpool skipper who lived and breathed LFC for 12 years, winning the hearts of the nation along the way with his warm, beaming smile, particularly when he lifted the European Cup for the first time in 1977.

"Crazy Horse" – as he was nicknamed – was a non-stop defender who could pass, tackle and score the odd important goal, all with the same infectious enthusiasm he had every time he pulled on a red shirt. One of the club's greatest captains, he is remembered as a club legend for his many achievements at Anfield.

GAMES and GOALS

League 474 35
FA Cup 62 1
League Cup 46 3
Europe 79 10
Other 4 0
Total .... **665** **49**

TROPHIES

First Division x 4
European Cup x 2
FA Cup x 1
FA Charity Shield x 3

UEFA Cup x 2
UEFA Super Cup x 1

He absolutely adored playing football. He would just give 110 per cent. They called him Crazy Horse and that's exactly what he was. He never stopped, he was up and down the pitch, cajoling everyone. He'll not be forgotten.

TERRY McDERMOTT

In our Liverpool days, if you were feeling low on confidence, you needed a player like him in your side. The bigger the game, the better he was.

JOHN TOSHACK

You couldn't not sign for him. He believed so much in what he did. The big fallacy about Shanks was that he was a great coach. He wasn't, but he was a great manager. He knew how to motivate.

EMLYN HUGHES

on Bill Shankly

I was fortunate to be the first captain to win the European Cup in 1977 – the first Liverpool had won and Bill Shankly had been planning that since 1962!

EMLYN HUGHES

Phil Thompson
1971 – 1984

Phil Thompson was arguably the first of a new style of centre-back who preferred to bring the ball out of defence and pass it out from the back rather than simply lump it down field.

Both Bill Shankly and Bob Paisley nurtured Thompson's ability, and he rewarded them with consistency and a love of the club that was apparent in everything he did in a Liverpool shirt. The reward for his efforts was to lead the Reds to European Cup glory for a third time in 1981 – one of many highs during a career at Anfield that spanned one of the most successful periods in LFC history.

GAMES and GOALS

League 340 7
FA Cup 36 0
League Cup 43 1
Europe 50 5
Other 8 0
Total .... **477** **13**

TROPHIES

First Division x 4
FA Cup x 1
FA Charity Shield x 3

European Cup x 2
UEFA Cup x 2
UEFA Super Cup x 1

Phil is the best back-four player in the country.
He reads the game brilliantly and never panics no
matter what.

EMLYN HUGHES

It was like telepathy. Neither of us
could head it, neither of us could tackle, my
missus was quicker than he was,
but we did alright.

ALAN HANSEN

on his partnership with Thompson

For me, a boy from the Kop, to lead Liverpool out, on the night they won the title, at Anfield, was a fabulous feeling.

PHIL THOMPSON

Shanks was the father figure but Roger Hunt was something special. It might sound daft but just picking up his sweaty kit gave me satisfaction.

PHIL THOMPSON

Ron Yeats
1961 – 1971

When Liverpool needed a man-mountain seemingly constructed of granite, Bill Shankly turned to gnarly Scottish centre-back Ron Yeats, paying £20,000 to bring the defender in from Dundee United.

Yeats would pay back the faith by demanding nothing less than total commitment from his team-mates. After he'd signed, Shankly invited journalists to "come in and walk around him".

Nicknamed "The Colossus", few captains led the team more proudly than Yeats, who inspired the Reds to become one of the best teams of the sixties and he would go on to make 454 appearances during a decade of excellence at Anfield.

GAMES and GOALS

League 358 13
FA Cup 50 0
League Cup 7 0
Europe 36 2
Other 3 1
Total .... **454** **16**

TROPHIES

First Division x 2
Second Division x 1
FA Cup x 1
FA Charity Shield x 3

Big Ronny is the best centre-half I have ever seen. With him in the team and at his best, we used to think we were unbeatable. In the air he was great. Some people used to think he was weak on the ground, but I never saw anybody give him a chasing. He was the right man for captain.

ROGER HUNT

Take a walk around my centre-half, gentlemen, He's a colossus! Go on, walk round him. He's a colossus.

BILL SHANKLY

introduces new signing Yeats to the press...

I'm absolutely knackered!

RON YEATS

*tells Her Majesty Queen Elizabeth II how he's feeling
after leading Liverpool to a first-ever FA Cup triumph over
Leeds United in 1965*

Being the captain that took the club out of the
Second Division after eight years was a very, very
proud moment. We won the league by eight or
nine points that season, and to follow that by
being the first captain of Liverpool to lift the
FA Cup is something I am very proud of. I do not
go round with the medals on my chest, it is just
there for me to say.

RON YEATS

Chris Lawler
1960 – 1975

Nicknamed "The Silent Knight", Chris Lawler was an elegant right-back who supported the attack with great aplomb and had a knack of scoring vital goals, too, notching 61 in 549 appearances.

Dependable and economic in possession, another Shankly favourite – an accolade in itself! – Lawler would spend 15 seasons with the club he joined aged 17, clocking up more than 500 appearances and being part of a Liverpool team that would progress from the Second Division to champions of England during an incredible career.

GAMES and GOALS

League	406	41
FA Cup	47	4
League Cup	27	5
Europe	66	11
Other	3	0
Total	**549**	**61**

TROPHIES

First Division x 3

UEFA Cup x 1

FA Cup x 2

FA Community Shield x 4

What a goal-scoring full-back. They used to call him "the ghost". He could turn up anywhere, unexpected, and score vital goals. I think his ratio of games and goals is fantastic for a full-back and will never be beaten.

IAN CALLAGHAN

Lawler has proved himself the greatest-ever match-winning full-back in the business with nearly 50 goals. A fantastic achievement when you realise he hasn't scored any of them from the penalty-spot, or even direct from a free-kick. I can't believe there is a player who would complain if Lawler was voted Footballer of the Year. His consistency has earned him respect in every dressing room in the First Division.

BILL SHANKLY

I could have gone to Manchester United. Could have gone to Everton... I was one of 15 children. There was 11 boys and the whole family were Reds. I was the third youngest. So they wouldn't let me go to Everton. So my dad did say to me, 'Go up there (to Everton). You're not going to sign for them, but they might give you a pair of boots to try and bribe you!' And he was right. I got a brand new pair of Adidas football boots.

CHRIS LAWLER

Shankly said, 'I've got an idea. Leave it with me.' So in the next few weeks Ronnie Moran was coming to the end of his career and Gerry Byrne was playing right-back. So he moved Gerry Byrne over to left-back and tried me at right-back. I just played nearly every game after that.

CHRIS LAWLER

Virgil van Dijk

2018 – present day

Virgil van Dijk sits comfortably among the pantheon of legendary Liverpool defenders. Arguably one of the best centre-backs in Europe for a decade or more, the calm authority, fierce competitiveness and leadership van Dijk has shown are integral to all the successes the club has had since he joined.

Few get the better of the Dutch star, who was one of the first names on Jürgen Klopp's team-sheet and has become indispensable for Arne Slot. It is testament to van Dijk's ability that he could have fitted comfortably into any of the great Liverpool sides of years gone by.

GAMES and GOALS*

League 219 19
FA Cup 11 2
League Cup 10 2
Europe 56 3
Other 4 0
Total .... **300** **26**

* as of 31/01/2025

TROPHIES

Premier League x 1
FA Cup x 1
League Cup x 2
FA Community Shield x 1

Champions League x 1
UEFA Super Cup x 1
FIFA World Cup x 1

He's good on the pitch, good in the dressing room. Anyone who can offer these traits are right up there and he very rarely ever made a mistake.

MARK LAWRENSON

Virgil's arrival was obviously a big day in our common history. We wanted Virgil in the summer [of 2017]. For some reasons we couldn't do the transfer at that moment but then in the winter we tried again and could get it through. It was a very important day; it changed a lot for us.

JÜRGEN KLOPP

"

Over the years, I've worn the captaincy armband. Leading out the boys was a special feeling, whether it was European games or league or cup games. But when I was named the actual captain, that's special... I would've never thought [about] that when I was younger, which makes it maybe even more beautiful. I'm really blessed.

"

VIRGIL VAN DIJK

"

First and foremost, pressure is a privilege. You should embrace it, and you should enjoy it. I think at a club like Liverpool, it's absolutely normal. I want to be the best each and every game. I want to get the maximum out of myself, and that's something I really enjoy. I embrace it, make the most of it and enjoy it as well.

"

VIRGIL VAN DIJK

Sami Hyypiä
1999 – 2009

For many Liverpool fans, Sami Hyypiä is a modern-day great. Joining in 1999 from Dutch side Willem II, the Finnish defender would quickly gain cult status at Anfield with his commanding, no-nonsense defending and it wasn't long before he was an integral member of the Reds' starting XI – the rock of the back four.

Hyypiä would go on to clock up almost 500 appearances during a decade of sterling service, and many believe the £2.6m fee Liverpool paid represents one of the best pieces of business the club has ever made.

GAMES and GOALS

League	318	22
FA Cup	29	2
League Cup	19	3
Europe	94	8
Other	4	0
Total	**464**	**35**

TROPHIES

FA Cup x 2

League Cup x 2

FA Community Shield x 2

Champions League x 1

UEFA Super Cup x 2

It's difficult to put into words how we
feel about Sami. He's been fantastic for us, a
colossus. He certainly deserves legendary status
and he is definitely one of the best players I have
ever played alongside.

STEVEN GERRARD

One of the best bits of business we've done over
the years... a steal – a bargain.

RON YEATS
LFC legend and chief scout at the time Hyypiä joined

It will only be after I've left, I'll be able to
sit back and realise what we've done in my
10 years. It is hard to take in now. It is nice to be
remembered here.

SAMI HYYPIÄ

Joining Liverpool was a dream come true.

SAMI HYYPIÄ

Alan Kennedy
1978 – 1986

When you think of the marauding full-backs – or even wing-backs – of today, you need look no further than the blueprint set by Alan Kennedy.

Signed from Newcastle United in 1978 by Bob Paisley, the left-back would spend eight glorious years at Anfield. He had the knack of scoring some huge goals, twice effectively scoring the winner in the European Cup final – one in open play against Real Madrid in 1981, and from the penalty spot in the resulting shoot-out with Roma in 1984.

Many feel the two England caps he won were scant reward for a player who gave wonderful service to an excellent Liverpool side.

GAMES and GOALS

League	251	15
FA Cup	21	0
League Cup	45	2
Europe	36	3
Other	6	0
Total	**359**	**20**

TROPHIES

First Division x 5

League Cup x 4

FA Community Shield x 3

European Cup x 2

You'd go short and he'd hit it long. You'd go long and he'd hit it short. I used to say: 'Alan, you took five years off my career.'

RAY KENNEDY

That was the beauty of playing with Alan, you never, ever knew where he was going to be.

ALAN HANSEN

I had planned all the way through the shoot-out to put the ball to the keeper's left but changed my mind during the run-up and put it to his right. I had also planned, if I scored, to do a wonderful cartwheel/somersault celebration but I was so carried away that I just ended up running, running and, eventually, jumping up in the air, like a madman!

ALAN KENNEDY

explains his thinking after securing another European Cup success

My first game was against Queens Park Rangers at Anfield... I miskicked with my right foot – the one I use for standing on – and knocked a policeman's helmet off. I also conceded a couple of corners and made a few errors. I just wanted half-time to come to get some reassurance from the manager, but when I got back to the dressing room, Bob [Paisley] said to me, 'I think that they shot the wrong Kennedy!'

ALAN KENNEDY

Trent Alexander-Arnold

2016 – present day

A unique, homegrown talent who has gone on to become one of the best right-backs in the world, Trent Alexander-Arnold is also one of the most gifted passers to ever play for Liverpool.

A cultured right-back who has clocked up more than 300 appearances for the Reds, TAA's passing range is up there with the very best and has led him to often be deployed in midfield. The big conundrum is where Alexander-Arnold's best position actually is, but his quick-thinking and ability to cut a defence to shreds with a penetrating, pinpoint pass – along with his lethal ability from dead-ball situations – make him a full-back like no other currently in world football.

GAMES and GOALS*

League 247 16
FA Cup 13 1
League Cup 10 0
Europe 66 3
Other 4 1
Total .... **340** **21**

as of 31/01/2025

TROPHIES

Premier League x 1
FA Cup x 1
League Cup x 2
FA Community Shield x 1

Champions League x 1
UEFA Super Cup x 1
FIFA Club World Cup x 1

He's the best passer of a ball at right-back that I've ever seen. He's David Beckham and Kevin De Bruyne at right-back.

GARY NEVILLE

I've seen him in the last seven years growing and developing as a player and as a man. It's clear that at this club you need a specific DNA. If not him then who could have that? He knows how I value him. We have had similar conversations about that in the past. I could imagine for a boy from West Derby it's a big thing for him and his family, but it's not because of that. It's because of his personality. He deserves it.

JÜRGEN KLOPP

on TAA's promotion to vice-captain

I live the dream every day really. Being able to represent the club and to be in and around names and players, and obviously managers and staff, that are world class every day is a privilege for me and I'm very fortunate to be in the position I am.

TRENT ALEXANDER-ARNOLD

Growing up you never think you will win all these trophies. You see legendary players who do that, and you think it is unbelievable. To be able to say I have done that at such a young age is a dream come true and it is motivation to go on and carry on winning more trophies. Hopefully there is a lot more to come.

TRENT ALEXANDER-ARNOLD

Andy Robertson

2017 – present day

One of the defining elements of the Jürgen Klopp era was having two dynamic full-backs racing down either flank. On one side during Klopp's reign was Trent Alexander-Arnold – on the other was Andy Robertson.

The Scottish left-back's arrival in 2017 was unheralded and little was known about him, but if his first campaign was mainly about bedding in, by his second Robertson was among the most coveted defenders in the Premier League.

Fast, whole-hearted and feisty, it's no wonder he became such a huge fan favourite at Anfield, and he has gone on to be regarded as one of the very best left-backs the club has ever had – and all for a bargain £8 million!

GAMES and GOALS*

League	239	10
FA Cup	11	0
League Cup	9	0
Europe	62	1
Other	5	0
Total	**326**	**11**

as of 31/01/2025

TROPHIES

Premier League x 1
FA Cup x 1
League Cup x 2
FA Community Shield x 1

Champions League x 1
UEFA Super Cup x 1
FIFA Club World Cup x 1

I am still tired just looking at Robertson. He makes 100-metre sprints every minute, absolutely incredible, and these are qualities.

JOSÉ MOURINHO

the then Manchester United boss reflects on Robertson's role in a 3–1 defeat

One thing that calls my attention is that he's always improving, he's not comfortable in his situation being first choice. The two full-backs of Liverpool right now are unbelievable. We can contest in any kind of way.

FÁBIO AURÉLIO

the former Liverpool full-back praising Robertson

My attitude when I go on to the pitch has always been fearless. I've never gone into a game fearing anything or anyone.

ANDY ROBERTSON

I always believe if we all give 100 per cent, some days not everything will come off for you – you'll have bad touches, mistimed tackles – but if I've given 100 per cent, you'll still get criticised and you'll criticise yourself in terms of performance, but you'll know you've made it hard for your opponent. That's the attitude I've always taken and will always continue to have.

ANDY ROBERTSON

Jamie Carragher

1996 – 2013

The fact that Jamie Carragher spent his entire career with Liverpool, enjoying 17 seasons and 737 appearances in the process, tells you all you need to know about this bona fide LFC legend.

Loyalty and longevity are two key words when talking about Carragher. Strong, adaptable and consistent, he was a centre-back who could have comfortably played in any of the great LFC sides over the years. His work-rate and will to win were other standout attributes, and he loved nothing more than a crunching – but fair – tackle. Carragher was a terrific leader and organiser and a superb reader of the game, too.

GAMES and GOALS

League 508 4
FA Cup 40 0
League Cup 35 0
Europe................... 150 1
Other 4 0
Total................. **737** **5**

TROPHIES

FA Cup x 2
League Cup x 3
FA Community Shield x 2

Champions League x 1
UEFA Cup x 1
UEFA Super Cup x 2
FIFA Club World Cup x 1

He was ultra-competitive and probably the most driven footballer I have ever met.

JAMIE REDKNAPP

Carragher is 10 times a better defender than I could ever be. He is a completely different player. He is a great defender whereas I was not. My strengths were on the ball, positional sense and recovery pace. The way he held Chelsea at bay was unbelievable. I'm sitting there in awe of how many times he intercepted, blocked and covered. I think if we look at Liverpool greats over the years – and there have been a lot of them – Carragher is up there with the best of them.

ALAN HANSEN

There may be more skilful players in the squad,
but no one can ever say I don't give 100 per cent.

JAMIE CARRAGHER

I'd plummeted to the deepest pit of misery, only
to instantly recover to ascend the highest of
peaks... no footballer fancies a sneak preview of
the most humiliating defeat in sporting history. But
having staged a comeback that will echo in
eternity, none of us would want it any other way.

JAMIE CARRAGHER

on Liverpool's incredible 2005 Champions League win over AC Milan

CHAPTER
3

THE GREATEST MIDFIELDERS

From world class playmakers to ferocious tacklers and personalities – plus everything in-between – Liverpool have been blessed with a mixture of silk and steel midfielders over the years...

Ray Kennedy
1974 – 1982

A graceful, intelligent central midfielder who would have slotted into any team anywhere during the 1970s, Ray Kennedy was a mainstay of a wonderful Liverpool side. A great passer, his timing was also immaculate, especially when arriving on the edge of the box, where he tucked away a number of sweet strikes during his career.

After winning the Double with Arsenal, Kennedy was Bill Shankly's parting gift to LFC – and what a gift this classiest of midfielders proved to be during a trophy-laden eight-year stay at Anfield.

GAMES and GOALS

League 275 51
FA Cup 28 3
League Cup 35 6
Europe 50 12
Other 5 0
Total .... **393** **72**

TROPHIES

First Division x 5
League Cup x 1
FA Charity Shield x 4

European Cup x 3
UEFA Cup x 1
European Super Cup x 1

Ray played in no man's land, in a world of his own, but he gave the team balance. He had style and he reminded me of Matt Busby. Ray Kennedy was some player.

BILL SHANKLY

Tactically Ray was in a different league. He had a delicate touch; a sweet left foot and his movement was phenomenal. I used to cover much more ground and tackle more, and he'd cover less ground but use his head more. We worked well together. His best point has to be his timing. I'd have the ball, I'd look up and he was gone. A perfectly timed run, ghosting in from the left, losing his marker. I'd put in the simplest of balls and bang! One nil.

JIMMY CASE

Fines, court appearances, jail... we were bad for each other. We had a bit of fun, but we did it at the right time. At hotels, when we asked for the room key, the receptionist would dive under the desk and say: 'Not you two!' Everyone has a pal, but Jim and I went deeper than that. If something went wrong, one of us sorted it out. It was a good friendship.

RAY KENNEDY
on close pal Jimmy Case

I had Alan Kennedy playing with me... When people asked which Kennedy I was I'd say, 'The intelligent one.'

RAY KENNEDY

Terry McDermott
1974 – 1982

Terry McDermott could be labelled as a Frank Lampard-style star of the 1970s. A pivotal midfielder who would score at least 10 goals per season from centre mid – and often more than that – he patrolled the edge of the opposition penalty area waiting for scraps, which were often dispatched with venom into the back of the net.

A man who perfected the art of the late run, McDermott didn't get the England recognition his performances merited, but at Anfield, with his shaggy perm and moustache, he was a Kop hero who had a bit of everything.

GAMES and GOALS

League	232	54
FA Cup	23	4
League Cup	36	5
Europe	34	15
Other	4	3
Total	**329**	**81**

TROPHIES

First Division x 5
League Cup x 2
FA Charity Shield x 4

European Cup x 3
UEFA Cup x 1
UEFA Super Cup x 1

Terry's strengths were running, passing and finishing. Along with his vision, Terry had another great quality: he was always upbeat. The banter at Liverpool was unbelievable, particularly when Terry Mac was in full flow.

KENNY DALGLISH

Off the field he was one of the biggest jokers we have had and a man who enjoyed a pint or two. But no matter how well he celebrated he was always in at training the following morning and that is all that mattered to Liverpool Football Club.

BOB PAISLEY

"

I was in the player's lounge and the payphone rang. It was a reporter. He told me and I gave my famous quote: 'I can't believe a ragbag like me has won a trophy like this.' Look at all the players before me, like George Best, Billy Bremner and Norman Hunter, who have all won these awards but never done it in the one year.

"

TERRY McDERMOTT

the Reds' midfielder recalls when he became the first footballer to win the PFA and FWA awards in one season

"

I used to enjoy my football. The camaraderie in the dressing room was superb and that's so important. We were by far the best team for a lot of years. When you look back at it, bloody hell, the team that we had, no wonder nobody could beat us. We knew we were the best team in the country, if not in Europe.

"

TERRY McDERMOTT

Jimmy Case

1973 – 1981

Jimmy Case was a fearsome presence on the football pitch. A player with a shot like a cannonball, he marauded the Reds' midfield like a terrier, and his superb goal in the 1977 FA Cup final proved he was more than just a tough nut who added a touch of steel to the silk of players like Kenny Dalglish and Ray Kennedy.

Case was a man of his time – pushing the boundaries to the limit and often winning duels by reputation alone. A vital cog in a team of winners.

GAMES and GOALS

League 186 23
FA Cup 22 7
League Cup 22 3
Europe 35 13
Other 4 0
Total .... **269** **46**

TROPHIES

First Division x 4
League Cup x 1
FA Charity Shield x 4

European Cup x 3
UEFA Cup x 1
European Super Cup x 1

I won't say he was dirty but certainly the hardest opponent was Jimmy Case. He could certainly look after himself. He was very clever about it as well.

BRYAN ROBSON

That Case boy, he's got some aggression, hasn't he? I think we'll have some of that.

JOE FAGAN

after chastising Case for punching Alec Lindsay!

I had someone in the old Kemlyn Road stand saying: 'Hey Jimmy, are you hungry?' He's got a pie in his hand. 'Do you wanna bite?' I had a little bite before giving it back and then carried on.

JIMMY CASE

I ended up finishing my career playing at Brighton and I was 41 and a half, and I left Liverpool when I was 27 or 28. I think it was just that – without being controversial – you get in a few scrapes, you're breathalysed and you're caught fighting in a hotel in Wales like me and Ray Kennedy were, and the club didn't look upon that too kindly.

JIMMY CASE

on why his days at Anfield ended perhaps sooner than they should have

Tommy Smith

1962 – 1978

Known as "The Anfield Iron", and with good reason, Tommy Smith was very much old school and like a stick of rock. You could have cut him open, and it would have said Liverpool inside.

Smith cut a formidable figure in the centre of the park with a sneering glance often enough to send opposition players into a panic. Smith represented his boyhood heroes for 16 years and was selected continuously by both Shankly and Paisley – though his job was largely to break up play and spoil, he'd contribute all over the park during one of the club's most glorious eras.

GAMES and GOALS

League	467	36
FA Cup	52	2
League Cup	30	2
Europe	85	8
Other	4	0
Total	**638**	**48**

TROPHIES

First Division x 4

FA Cup x 2

FA Charity Shield x 4

European Cup x 2

UEFA Cup x 2

UEFA Super Cup x 1

Tommy hated losing and was quite prepared to put himself through all manner of pain and suffering to avoid it. There was an element of notoriety about it which I think he quite enjoyed, but if any opponent cared to put that reputation to the test, Tommy didn't disappoint them. His fearless nature not only unsettled the opposition, it inspired his team-mates.

BOB PAISLEY

'Come near me and I'll break yer back', was his catchphrase. But he's actually a very nice man, honest!

NORMAN HUNTER

I make no bones about it, that's what I was good at. Some players were good dribblers, others good headers, I was a hard tackler, and I used it to gain that 'edge' that Shanks was always looking for.

TOMMY SMITH

There is a famous picture of me after the final whistle running towards Ronnie Moran. It looks as if I was dashing across to throw my arms around him, but in fact I was asking for my two false teeth. I had to look the part in the post-match photo session.

TOMMY SMITH

on the celebrations after the European final in 1977

Graeme Souness
1978 – 1984

Something close to what many would consider the perfect midfielder, Graeme Souness had it all. A magnificent passer of the ball, a ferocious tackler and an ability to score thunderous shots from distance, there was nothing this man couldn't do with a football.

Silk and steel with a nasty side to his game, he was a born winner and the beating heart of Liverpool for six years, during which time he earned the adulation of the Kop in the process – no mean feat. One of the best players of his generation.

GAMES and GOALS

League	247	38
FA Cup	24	2
League Cup	45	9
Europe	38	6
Other	5	0
Total	**359**	**55**

TROPHIES

First Division x 5

League Cup x 4

FA Charity Shield x 3

European Cup x 3

I nutmegged Souness once in training. He just laughed, but then a few years later I did the same thing against him in a match, and he elbowed me in the face.

KEVIN SHEEDY

When you're walking behind Souness and he's walking towards the enemy, 30-40,000 of them, with a big smile on his face – he actually wants to climb the fence and stand even closer to them – there's only one thing that happens. Your chest goes out and you just want to get in there as well. When you're playing for a captain like that and playing alongside a guy who was not just a great captain but a great player... what team do I want to play for? I think I'll take that one.

STEVE NICOL

"

Being successful has always been more important to me than being popular. I long ago accepted that the name of Graeme Souness would top few popularity polls... you could say that I have achieved my ambition for, thanks to Liverpool, I have a cupboard full of memories and scarcely a friend on the terraces or in the dressing room.

"

GRAEME SOUNESS

"

That first day at Anfield, 10 January 1978, was a revelation... no prima donnas, no superstars. I made only one error on that first morning, I asked Tommy Smith if I could borrow his hairdryer (hard to imagine but it's absolutely true) and he turned to Phil Neal and said pointedly: 'Everyone is allowed one mistake'. I took my own in the future.

"

GRAEME SOUNESS

Steven Gerrard

1998 – 2015

In the list of all-time Liverpool legends, Steven Gerrard sits comfortably at the top table. With 17 years of magnificent service, the boyhood Red would only have one gap on his CV – a Premier League title, which is a genuine shame given his loyalty and leadership.

A captain fantastic in every way imaginable, "Stevie G" was a magnificent footballer and a generational talent. His ability to create and score spectacular goals made him a unique footballer – one who will never be forgotten on the Kop. The figures speak for themselves: 185 goals, 145 assists in 710 appearances.

GAMES and GOALS

League	504	120
FA Cup	42	15
League Cup	30	9
Europe	130	41
Other	4	1
Total	**710**	**186**

TROPHIES

FA Cup x 2
League Cup x 3
FA Community Shield x 1

Champions League x 1
UEFA Cup x 1
UEFA Super Cup x 1

Nobby Stiles once told me that he thought Steven Gerrard was the nearest thing to Duncan Edwards and that is a tremendous compliment for a player. His all-action displays constantly put pressure on the opposition and he must be the best midfielder in the world at present.

TOMMY SMITH

Gerrard has become the most influential player in England, bar none. To me, Gerrard is Keane; he is now where Keane was when Roy came to us in 1994. I've watched him quite a lot, and everywhere the ball is, he seems to be there. He's got that unbelievable engine, desire, determination. Anyone would take Gerrard.

SIR ALEX FERGUSON

I'd just like to say that I'm delighted to
be captain of Liverpool Football Club and I'm
thrilled to be representing the fans on the pitch.
Hopefully I can lift a trophy this season to say
thanks for all the support from fans everywhere.

STEVEN GERRARD

It means the world for me to play for this club.
I would sign for the rest of my career if Liverpool
want me to.

STEVEN GERRARD

Philippe Coutinho
2013 – 2018

At a time when Liverpool weren't winning trophies, Philippe Coutinho was undoubtedly a shining light. The Brazilian attacking midfielder was signed in January 2013 for just £8.5 million from Inter Milan and his arrival largely went under the radar, but his performances soon made him an instant crowd idol.

Dynamic, exciting and with the ability to score spectacular goals, Coutinho graced the Reds' midfield for five and a half seasons, before moving to Barcelona for a club record close to £150 million – quite a return given the entertainment and pleasure he provided during his stay on Merseyside.

GAMES and GOALS

League	152	41
FA Cup	13	4
League Cup	12	2
Europe	24	7
Total	**201**	**54**

TROPHIES

None

Stay here and they will end up building
a statue in your honour. Go somewhere else, to
Barcelona, to Bayern Munich, to Real Madrid, and
you will be just another player. Here you can be
something more.

JÜRGEN KLOPP

I think everyone knows what a great footballer Phil
is, that is not in question – but not everyone sees
what an incredibly positive character he is and
what a big influence he is on the dressing room.

JÜRGEN KLOPP

Hopefully I will have a long career
at Liverpool.

PHILIPPE COUTINHO

I'm feeling very happy, it's a very important step
in my career. Liverpool is a great club with great
players. We've always heard about Liverpool's
history in Brazil. I know they believe in me
and my football.

PHILIPPE COUTINHO

Ronnie Whelan

1979 – 1994

In a Liverpool career that spanned three decades, Ronnie Whelan's contribution to the Reds was huge. The Irish midfielder joined the club for just £35,000 from Home Farm and would give 14 wonderful years of service, eventually going on to captain the team.

Whelan was unflashy, hard-working and got on with his job, but with 73 goals and 42 assists while at Anfield – many of those goal contributions in big games – Whelan was a crucial member of Bob Paisley and later Kenny Dalglish's sides. A wonderful, dedicated and loyal club servant.

GAMES and GOALS

League	362	46
FA Cup	41	7
League Cup	50	14
Europe	24	6
Other	16	0
Total	**493**	**73**

TROPHIES

First Division x 6

FA Cup x 3

League Cup x 3

FA Charity Shield x 4

European Cup x 1

And when those special matches come round and there are medals to be won and the pundits are asking whether the match winner will be Rushy or Kenny or Brucie, then I look past them all towards Ronnie Whelan and think to myself: 'There's our man for the big occasion.'

BOB PAISLEY

He came over from Ireland as a young boy at 18 years of age. Scored on his debut against Stoke City I think and just carried on from there. A good goalscorer, good passer and good runner. A determined and hard midfield player who was very underrated.

KENNY DALGLISH

"

I didn't try to do anything spectacular. I couldn't dribble. I was a good passer of the ball. I could read the game well. I could break up attacks and start them off very quickly. The managers and the players appreciated the job more than some of the supporters.

"

RONNIE WHELAN

"

I went to Liverpool in the summer for a two-week trial and by June-July they decided they wanted to keep me. I was pretty nervous about going there but my dad told me I might as well start at the top!

"

RONNIE WHELAN

Jordan Henderson
2011 – 2023

Though not perhaps appreciated by the wider football public, Jordan Henderson will forever have the admiration and respect of Liverpool supporters.

Signed from Sunderland as a raw 21-year-old, he couldn't have predicted that he would go on to spend the next 13 seasons at Anfield, captaining the side for much of the time, and leading the side to European and domestic glory in the process. Henderson knew his job – work tirelessly each and every game, lead the team by example and drive his team-mates on and off the pitch. A wonderful club servant.

GAMES and GOALS

League	360	29
FA Cup	26	0
League Cup	28	1
Europe	74	3
Other	4	0
Total	**492**	**33**

TROPHIES

Premier League x 1
FA Cup x 1
League Cup x 2
FA Community Shield x 1

Champions League x 1
UEFA Super Cup x 1
FIFA Club World Cup x 1

Teams can't function at Liverpool's level without a cog like Jordan Henderson.

STEVEN GERRARD

Yes, he is exceptional. Yes, he is outstanding.
If anybody who's with us still doesn't see the quality of Jordan Henderson, then I can't help him.
Is Hendo the perfect football player? No.
Do I know anybody who is? No. Is he unbelievably important to us? Yes!

JÜRGEN KLOPP

"

Just know, I will always be a Red,
until the day I die.

"

JORDAN HENDERSON

"

I can't lie, there have been hard times, really
hard times. But when I look back at my career at
Liverpool, it will always be the good times that
I remember.

"

JORDAN HENDERSON

CHAPTER

4

THE GREATEST FORWARDS

Liverpool have been blessed with some truly wonderful forwards over the years.

Exceptional goal-scorers, skilful technicians and goal-poachers par excellence. Here are the best of the best to wear that treasured red shirt...

Peter Thompson
1963 – 1973

Peter Thompson was a cultured winger who Bill Shankly played throughout his Anfield tenure, though his last three years at the club were spent mainly out of the starting XI. Everton legend Dixie Dean once admitted he would have loved to have played alongside Thompson and Ian Callaghan saying that if he had, he would have scored even more than the 60 league goals he managed in one incredible season for the Toffees.

Technically brilliant, skilful and a terrific crosser, Thompson was a first-team regular for almost a decade and was twice in the 28-man squad for both the 1966 and 1970 World Cups, ultimately not making the final 22-man squads on both occasions.

GAMES and GOALS

League	322	41
FA Cup	38	5
League Cup	9	2
Europe	44	6
Other	3	0
Total	**416**	**54**

TROPHIES

First Division x 2

FA Charity Shield x 3

If I could play between Ian Callaghan
and Peter Thompson, I'd still get my
60 goals a season.

DIXIE DEAN
legendary Everton goal-machine

His work rate was outstanding, his fitness
unequalled, his balance like a ballet dancer. I have
no hesitation in placing Peter up among the
all-time greats – alongside such players as Tom
Finney, Stanley Matthews and George Best.
They say he didn't score enough goals; they said
his final pass wasn't telling enough. Well, if he
had scored goals as well as everything else he
did, he would have been in the same category as
Jesus Christ!

BILL SHANKLY

Mr Shankly took me all around Melwood.
He showed me Anfield. Took me to the office.
The Chairman came in: 'Could you sign here?'
'Actually Mr. Shankly, I would like a signing-on fee.'
'You what? I am giving you the chance to play in
the greatest city in the greatest team that is
going to be in the world, and you want illegal
money. Get out!' 'Give me the pen,' I said.
So I signed. Best thing I ever did.

PETER THOMPSON

on signing for Liverpool

Ian [Callaghan] and I were completely different.
I was an individualist. Ian was straightforward,
boring, pushing it down the line, cross it,
boom 1-0! How boring is that?

PETER THOMPSON

Ian Callaghan
1959 – 1978

Liverpool's record appearance holder, often under-rated and maybe even taken for granted by some, winger Ian Callaghan played throughout the Shankly and Paisley eras and was named on the team-sheet an amazing 857 times.

Initially a winger, he combined with Peter Thompson to provide a devastating wide attack for the Reds for many years. Callaghan was more direct than Thompson, understanding his job was to beat his man and get the ball in the middle. He moved into a more conventional midfield position as the years rolled on but never gave less than his best. A club great in every sense of the word.

GAMES and GOALS

League	640	49
FA Cup	79	2
League Cup	42	7
Europe	89	10
Other	7	0
Total	**857**	**68**

TROPHIES

First Division x 5
Second Division x 1
FA Cup x 2
FA Charity Shield x 6

European Cup x 2
UEFA Cup x 2
European Super Cup x 1

Ian Callaghan is everything good that a man can be. No praise is too high for him. Words cannot do justice to the amount he has contributed to the game. Ian Callaghan will go down as one of the game's truly great players.

BILL SHANKLY

There is a 17-year-old called Ian Callaghan who looks like taking over from me. I played with him twice, watched his progress and I believe he'll be a credit to his club, the game and his country.

BILLY LIDDELL

Everton were the glamour club back then, they had a much better stadium and I had a chance to go to them, but I was a Liverpool supporter and signing for them appealed to me more. The fact that two of my heroes, Alan A'Court and the great Billy Liddell, were here made it easy for me to sign.

IAN CALLAGHAN

I was an outside right until 1970 when I got my cartilage injury. I lost my place to John McLaughlin and then Brian Hall. When I got back I was put in central midfield and I probably enjoyed playing there more than when I was on the wing. I probably got more recognition playing in that role.

IAN CALLAGHAN

Ian St John

1961 – 1971

Another player who sweated blood for the cause of Liverpool FC, Ian St John was, like Ron Yeats, in at phase one of Bill Shankly's masterplan. Signed from Motherwell for £37,500, he was a selfless striker who forged a formidable, hard-working partnership with Roger Hunt.

St John wore the shirt with pride during a memorable decade at Anfield. During this time, he led the line for the Reds, notching more than a century of goals and assists, underlining his importance to Liverpool's renaissance and eventual dominance of English football.

GAMES and GOALS

League	336	95
FA Cup	49	12
League Cup	6	1
Europe	32	10
Other	2	0
Total	**425**	**118**

TROPHIES

First Division x 2
Second Division x 1
FA Cup x 1
FA Charity Shield x 3

"

I didn't sign the best centre forward in the country... I signed the only centre-forward.

"

BILL SHANKLY

"

As far as I am concerned Ian was the kingpin of the side which achieved so much success in the sixties. Ian was a good strong player who knew what it was all about. He played two roles during his career, firstly up front when he was younger and then when he was older, he dropped into midfield and still played well. Along with Gordon Milne, I think Ian was the player who used to make Liverpool tick.

"

JOE MERCER

There's no noise like the Anfield
noise – and I love it!

IAN ST JOHN

I was sent off six times, but two of those were for
mistaken identity. The referees were blind in those
days as well.

IAN ST JOHN

Ian Rush

1980 – 1996

A prolific, instinctive goal-scorer of the highest order, Ian Rush signed for £300,000 from Chester and terrorised defences for the best part of 16 years. His partnership with Kenny Dalglish was among the deadliest in the history of the club.

Rush scored all kinds of goals but the majority he bagged were of the predatory nature, and if there was a loose ball in the box or a tap-in, Rush would inevitably be first there to stick the ball in the net. A natural goal-poacher and one of Liverpool's greatest strikers.

GAMES and GOALS

League	469	229
FA Cup	61	39
League Cup	78	48
Europe	38	20
Other	14	10
Total	**660**	**346**

TROPHIES

First Division x 5

FA Cup x 3

League Cup x 5

FA Charity Shield x 4

European Cup x 2

Records are there to be broken. I thought
it'd last a bit longer when he went to Italy but
then he came back! I wasn't gutted when he
resigned – if anyone had to break my
record, I'm glad it was Ian Rush.

ROGER HUNT

Ian Rush made me look brilliant in the air.
When I jumped up and headed, the ball would
always go to Rushie. He could read my body;
[from] the way I jumped up Ian would deduce
where the ball would go. He worked it out before
I had. Rush never knew which bloody knife or fork
to use, but on the pitch, he was a genius.

MICHAEL ROBINSON

It was an emotional day but also a fantastic day for me. The reception I got will live with me forever. I'm sorry I didn't score. The fans were willing me to score, and I wanted to score as much as they wanted me to. I wanted to stay on the pitch forever.

IAN RUSH

on his final game at Anfield in 1996

It's best being a striker. If you miss five then score the winner, you're a hero. The goalkeeper can play a blinder, then let one in... and he's a villain.

IAN RUSH

Roger Hunt

1958 – 1969

Signed from non-league Stockton Heath in 1958, Roger Hunt was a powerful striker who thrived off the crosses of Peter Thompson and Ian Callaghan. Hunt linked especially well with Ian St John to give Shankly's team a real cutting edge as they climbed towards the summit of English football.

Hunt, who had the honour of having one of his goals being the first ever seen on *Match of the Day*, played in the 1966 World Cup final and never let club or country down. It took goal-scoring phenomenon Ian Rush to finally break his overall goals record for the Reds.

GAMES and GOALS

League	404	244
FA Cup	44	18
League Cup	10	5
Europe	31	17
Other	3	1
Total	**492**	**285**

TROPHIES

First Division x 2
Second Division: x 1
FA Cup x 1
FA Charity Shield x 3

Roger Hunt is a player's player. He is possibly appreciated more by those who play with him and against him than by those who watch him.

SIR BOBBY MOORE

People talk about Keegan and Toshack or Rush and Dalglish when they are asked about great Liverpool striking duos, but I talk about Hunt and St John. When I pick my greatest ever Liverpool team, then Roger Hunt is the first forward I put in. We used to call him 'Over-the-bar Hunt'. Everyone used to get mail, praising you, calling you names or simply asking for an autograph. Roger used to get a letter on a regular basis from a lad, who clearly didn't like him. It always used to start. 'Dear Over-the-bar-Hunt. I see you missed another couple of sitters on Saturday.'

TOMMY SMITH

We knew that all other things being equal, like skill, tactics and run of the ball, it was fitness that would count in the end. So we kept at 100 per cent at all times, and it paid us. We have found that there is more satisfaction in a good win than there is in a pint or a cigarette packet.

ROGER HUNT

I knew perfectly well that I wasn't an out-and-out natural, the sort who can make a ball talk, so it was down to me to compensate for it in other ways. I made up my mind that if I didn't succeed at Anfield then it wouldn't be for the lack of determination. From the first day I threw myself into training, ran and tackled for everything and practised my ball skills at every opportunity.

ROGER HUNT

Billy Liddell
1938 – 1961

Look up the dictionary definition of "one-club man" and chances are there will be a picture of Billy Liddell next to it. A Kop legend who spent his entire career with the Reds and, but for the Second World War, he'd still be the club's record appearance holder.

Liddell was a prolific goal-scorer considering his position as a winger, and he finished top of the scoring charts eight times out of nine from 1949 to 1958. He was hugely popular, and, for a while, the Reds' nickname was 'Liddellpool' – high praise indeed. He stayed with the club for an incredible 22 years and will always be remembered as a Liverpool legend.

GAMES and GOALS

League 492 215
FA Cup 42 13
League Cup 0 0
Europe 0 0
Other 0 0
Total .... **534** **228**

TROPHIES

First Division x 1

Billy was so strong. His head and neck was all in one. This is my impression of him; I can remember him with two defenders hanging off him. He was so strong. With both feet, left or right, on the wing or centre-forward. He could play anywhere. Brilliant player.

GERRY BYRNE

Oh, what power! Opponents were frightened to death of the gentlest man on earth. Bill was so strong it was unbelievable. You couldn't shake him off the ball. It didn't matter where he was playing, though I suppose his best position was outside left. He could go round you, or past you, or even straight through you sometimes!

BOB PAISLEY

For five years as a schoolboy I used to play rugby every Saturday morning and soccer each afternoon, and all I could think of was that one day I might be good enough to play for Glasgow Rangers. Instead, Liverpool brought me south, and I've never regretted the day.

BILLY LIDDELL

Nothing is more certain than in the course of time we shall see a European league established.

BILLY LIDDELL

Kevin Keegan
1971 – 1977

A player loved by fans up and down the land, Kevin Keegan made a wonderful career out of what many would perhaps claim to be average ability – that's not to say he wasn't very good. He was a bundle of effervescent energy who was totally committed and deserved everything he got.

His partnership with John Toshack is the stuff of legend, and he left Anfield one of the most famous footballers on the planet and a national icon – perhaps the game's first superstar, even. Whatever Keegan lacked in height, he more than made up for in heart, courage and energy.

GAMES and GOALS

League	230	68
FA Cup	28	14
League Cup	23	6
Europe	40	12
Other	2	0
Total	**323**	**100**

TROPHIES

First Division x 3
FA Cup x 1
FA Charity Shield x 2

European Cup x 1
UEFA Cup x 2

Kevin Keegan was signed and made an unbelievable impact. He was the first superstar that Liverpool had. Kevin was a great player for Liverpool and I've nothing but admiration for him.

IAN CALLAGHAN

Kevin's sheer enthusiasm, bravery, fearless attitude and desire forced him into the team. First game of the season we beat Nottingham Forest 3–1 at home, and he was never out of the side after that.

RAY CLEMENCE

This was the perfect ending for me. I have played my last game for Liverpool. I have no regrets. It is a fantastic way to finish. I have only stayed on for this season because the club chairman asked me to stay to help to try to win the European Cup. I have kept my side of the bargain.

KEVIN KEEGAN

The self-appointed representative of the Kop came on the field to greet me... the smell of booze on his breath almost knocked me off my feet. The police accepted this ritual whenever there was a new player... He kissed me, then kissed the grass in front of the Kop and went back to join his mates in the crowd.

KEVIN KEEGAN

Kenny Dalglish
1977 – 1990

While Bill Shankly is the man Liverpool fans most identify with as a manager, Kenny Dalglish is the player the Kop will never forget. Like Shankly, this brilliant Scot tapped into the supporters' passion to the extent he became at one with them and for 13 years was one of the most cultured footballers in world football, let alone the First Division.

A wonderful individual player, a marvellous link-up player and true team man. Dalglish could have doubled his goals tally had he been more selfish, but his focus was always the team rather than personal glory. Who could forget his charismatic smile after a goal? A genuine club legend – the best of the best.

GAMES and GOALS

League	355	118
FA Cup	37	13
League Cup	59	27
Europe	51	11
Other	13	3
Total	**515**	**172**

TROPHIES

First Division x 6

FA Cup x 1

League Cup x 4

FA Charity Shield x 5

European Cup x 3

UEFA Super Cup x 1

I just hoped that after the trials and tribulations of my early years in management, someone up high would smile on me and guide my hand. My plea was answered when we got Kenny Dalglish. What a player, what a great professional!

BOB PAISLEY

Of all the players I have played alongside, managed and coached in more than 40 years at Anfield, he is the most talented. When Kenny shines, the whole team is illuminated.

BOB PAISLEY

Shanks said to me: 'I've got two pieces of advice for you – don't overeat in that hotel and don't lose your accent.'

KENNY DALGLISH

on the day he signed for Liverpool

There was only one Bob Paisley, and he was the greatest of them all... He could tell if someone was injured and what the problem was just by watching them walk a few paces. He was never boastful but had great football knowledge.
I owe Bob more than I owe anybody else in the game. There will never be another like him.

KENNY DALGLISH

Mo Salah

2017 – present day

There are modern day Liverpool legends – and then there is Mo Salah. "The Egyptian King" – as he is known at Anfield – is a certified superstar, not only on Merseyside but around the globe and particularly in his home nation.

He joined a select few when he surpassed the 200-goal mark for the Reds and has been prolific in each and every season he has been a Liverpool player. He formed one of the world's great strike forces when he played alongside Roberto Firmino and Sadio Mané and continued to score all kinds of goals when both players left. A talismanic figure, he will be remembered as a LFC great long after he has moved on.

GAMES and GOALS*

League 272 174
FA Cup 12 6
League Cup 9 3
Europe 83 50
Other 5 1
Total ....**381** **234**

* as of 31/01/2025

TROPHIES

Premier League x 1
FA Cup x 1
League Cup x 1
FA Community Shield x 1

Champions League x 1
UEFA Super Cup x 1
FIFA Club World Cup x 1

Look at what Cristiano Ronaldo has done to himself and how he has kept himself in prime condition. It's about attitude of mind, it's about living the right way, it's about applying yourself. The best example is Ronaldo ... and I think Mo is in that category.

RAY HOUGHTON

Mohamed has the perfect mix of experience and potential... His pace is incredible, he gives us more attacking threat. Most important, though, for us, is that he is hungry, willing and eager to be even better and improve further. He is an ambitious player who wants to win and win at the highest level.

JÜRGEN KLOPP

Ever since I was a kid, I had been a Liverpool fan
– they were my favourite Premier League club.

MO SALAH

I feel the love in the Liverpool club,
the city, and the training.

MO SALAH

Robbie Fowler
1993 – 2001 and 2006 – 2007

There have been few better finishers to represent Liverpool than Robbie Fowler – the man nicknamed 'God' on the Kop. The local lad made good, Fowler was, for several years, one of the best strikers in the world, with numbers to match.

For nine seasons he led the line for the Reds, topping 30 goals in all competitions on three occasions. Fowler could score all sorts of goals – tap-ins, long range efforts, headers, volleys... everything. Yet, despite playing for England and several other clubs, it was when he wore all red that he was at his most lethal, with Anfield his hunting ground. He returned for a second spell at LFC having left initially to join Leeds United and then Manchester City. A special talent.

GAMES and GOALS

Premier League	266	128
FA Cup	24	12
League Cup	35	29
Europe	44	14
Other	0	0
Total	**369**	**183**

TROPHIES

FA Cup x 1

League Cup x 2

UEFA Cup x 1

UEFA Super Cup x 1

I was watching my lad playing in goal for Ormskirk schoolboys against Liverpool schoolboys and this little lad knocked in two against him. I asked someone what his name was: 'Robbie Fowler'. From the start he was a fantastic talent.

ROY EVANS

He is often referred to as God, which sums up the respect he commands at Anfield from fans and players alike. But don't be surprised if he answers to Bernard, which is his other Christian name.

MICHAEL OWEN

After the Fulham game, I went round the chippy with my mates and got a big kiss from my mum when I got home!

ROBBIE FOWLER

after scoring five goals against Fulham in 1993

It is unbelievable, a dream come true.
I can hardly believe that I am back and it's an incredible feeling. After I'd signed, I sat in my car outside Anfield and was incredibly emotional.

ROBBIE FOWLER

on his return to Anfield in 2006

Sadio Mané
2016 – 2022

When Liverpool signed Senegalese forward Sadio Mané, few could have imagined the impact he'd have at the club. After scoring the winner on his debut against Arsenal, Mané never looked back, forging a lethal attack with Roberto Firmino and Mo Salah, making Liverpool's attack among the most feared in world football.

Mané's consistency was outstanding, with his appearances, goals and assists very similar each season throughout his six-year stay. With 120 goals in 269 appearances, it was no coincidence Liverpool had a 67 per cent win ratio with him in the team. Fast, aggressive and skilful – everything you'd want your forward to be.

GAMES and GOALS

League	196	90
FA Cup	8	4
League Cup	4	0
Europe	58	26
Other	3	0
Total	**269**	**120**

TROPHIES

Premier League x 1
FA Cup x 1
League Cup x 1

Champions League x 1
UEFA Super Cup x 1
FIFA Club World Cup x 1

I can't think of a single club anywhere in Europe that wouldn't want a player like Sadio available to them... He is such an important member of our team and squad. He radiates joy and I think this is reflected in his performances and impact on the pitch. The only criticism I could ever have of Sadio is that maybe at times he is the only one not to see just how good he is.

JÜRGEN KLOPP

Mané has fantastic attitude, he's a warrior and it would be far easier to say what he hasn't got... He's a fabulous player, there is nothing to dislike about him. He's smiley, open and you want to work with people like that. I think he'd be an absolute dream to work with.

IAN RUSH

I didn't dream about becoming a
professional: I dreamed about becoming
the best in the world.

SADIO MANÉ

There was interest from a lot of clubs, not just
Manchester United, but as soon as I knew
Liverpool were interested, I just felt it was the right
club with the right coach. It was right for me to
come here.

SADIO MANÉ

Michael Owen

1996 – 2004

Rarely has a talent exploded on to the English football scene in the way Michael Owen did for Liverpool. A precocious and prolific teenage goal-scorer, he broke into the first team as a 17-year-old and scored on his debut – it was the start of a wonderful Anfield spell that would jettison the Chester-born forward into super-stardom for club and country.

It is not an exaggeration to say that Owen was the most exciting discovery for decades, and he would go on to hit 20+ goals in five of his eight seasons with the Reds. A generational talent, his best years were undoubtedly at Anfield.

GAMES and GOALS

League	216	118
FA Cup	15	8
League Cup	14	9
Europe	50	22
Other	2	1
Total	**297**	**158**

TROPHIES

FA Cup x 1
League Cup x 2
FA Community Shield x 1

UEFA Cup x 1
UEFA Super Cup x 1

Roy Evans said to me, 'Karl, I have a new young talent that I want you to see.' And then, of course, I saw Michael playing in training, and I said to myself, 'This boy is not just a young talent, he is going to be a bloody great player!'

KARL-HEINZ RIEDLE

There's no reason why he will leave Liverpool and there's no reason why he should. Money isn't the be all and end all nowadays and Michael loves the club. If Michael was to stay at Liverpool for the rest of his career, he would become the all-time best-ever striker I think.

JOHN ALDRIDGE

It's important having a core of local lads in the side, especially for the fans. And if you play for Liverpool, you're a Liverpool fan.

MICHAEL OWEN

I genuinely felt like I had no equals, never felt like pressure.

MICHAEL OWEN

John Barnes
1987 – 1997

When John Barnes took the ball past Alan Hansen and scored for Watford, Kenny Dalglish knew he was a player he wanted in his team. In 1987, Liverpool paid £900,000 for the Jamaica-born winger, and Barnes would forge a lethal front three that included Peter Beardsley and John Aldridge.

It would be a trio that propelled the Reds to the league title – not to mention Barnes winning both the PFA Player of the Year and the FWA Footballer of the Year awards – and was the start of a wonderful decade for Barnes, who delivered on all his promise and plenty more. In a wonderful spell at Anfield, he would score and assist more than 200 goals in 407 appearances for the club.

GAMES and GOALS

League	314	84
FA Cup	51	16
League Cup	26	3
Europe	12	3
Other	4	2
Total	**407**	**108**

TROPHIES

First Division x 2
FA Cup x 2
League Cup x 1
FA Charity Shield x 3

Players like John Barnes come along
just once in a lifetime.

TOM FINNEY

John Barnes can be the greatest. He was
described by the England boss Bobby Robson
as the black [George] Best, and I reckon he is
right. Barnes has the ability to become the best,
the most exciting winger in British Soccer since
me. His transfer to Liverpool was the perfect move
for a man who was born with stunning talent.
The Anfield academy will take that natural ability,
harness it with consistency, and produce a
truly world-class performer.

GEORGE BEST

So what I didn't know was that in six years Liverpool had seen in me that I was able to translate that into what Liverpool wanted me to play. Liverpool saw things in players that you didn't know you had yourself.

JOHN BARNES

The people. I like the people. They're down to earth, they're humble. It was the same with the players of the past. You couldn't come to Liverpool with a superstar mentality, or believe you were better than anyone else in the team, or in the city. And I liked that.

JOHN BARNES

Luis Suárez
2011 – 2014

Emotive, explosive and exciting – three words that describe Uruguayan striker Luis Suárez and his memorable stay at Anfield. The four years at one club is a decent chunk of time, but such was Suárez's impact that his stay still feels like something of a cameo.

Suárez was unlike any Liverpool striker before him, able to score fantastic goals from anywhere and cause mayhem in opposition defences. A gifted footballer, he also had a short fuse that would get him into trouble on several occasions, with his temperament perhaps not all that it should have been. But for box office entertainment, he was a wonderful signing for the Reds.

GAMES and GOALS

League	110	69
FA Cup	9	5
League Cup	6	4
Europe	8	4
Other	0	0
Total	**133**	**82**

TROPHIES

League Cup x 1

I think that every defender in England hates
playing against him. He has a strong, provocative
personality. From the information I gathered on
him it appears that on a day-to-day level he is
really easy to work with. Also that he's respectful,
he loves training, he's an angel. He turns into a
demon when he's on the pitch. We all dream
about having players like that.

ARSÈNE WENGER

I'm delighted that he has signed. I think he's
one of the top strikers in world football.

BRENDAN RODGERS

Look, there's no rule in soccer against biting your opponent. There's not even a rule against eating your opponent. The only rule in soccer is that you can't use your hands.

LUIS SUÁREZ

It's a huge honour to wear No. 7 at Liverpool. I think about the legends: Dalglish, Keegan and that Australian guy.

LUIS SUÁREZ

CHAPTER
5

THE GREATEST MANAGERS

The best managers at Anfield have required charisma, genius and an ability to manage not only the players, but understand what Liverpool Football Club stands for...

Bill Shankly
1959 – 1974

Bill Shankly was the man who created two dynasties at Anfield and dragged LFC up by the scruff of its neck, while changing the whole ethos of the club in the process.

He was a manager who lived and breathed Liverpool Football Club from the moment he walked through the doors at Anfield, and a man who mapped out a successful blueprint that would ensure the Reds maintained a vice-like grip in England and in Europe.

If ever a club and manager were meant for each other it is Liverpool and Bill Shankly – a legend in every sense imaginable.

MANAGERIAL STATS

	PLD	W	D	L
League	609	319	152	138
FA Cup	75	40	22	13
League Cup	30	13	9	8
Europe	65	34	13	18
Other	5	2	2	1
Totals	**784**	**408**	**198**	**178**

TROPHIES

First Division x 3

Second Division x 1

FA Cup x 2

FA Charity Shield x 3

UEFA Cup x 1

I was like any other Liverpool fan, in awe of the
team and in awe of Bill Shankly. Everyone knew
that Shankly was creating a monster; this was no
ordinary football team.

PHIL THOMPSON

He was inspirational. If he told you, you were
going to hell, you would look forward to the trip.

KEVIN KEEGAN

Some people believe football is a matter of life
and death, I am very disappointed with that
attitude. I can assure you it is much, much more
important than that.

BILL SHANKLY

Bob [Paisley] and I never had any rows. We didn't
have any time for that. We had to plan where we
were going to keep all the cups we won.

BILL SHANKLY

Bob Paisley
1974 – 1983

Without doubt Liverpool's most successful manager and one of the greatest of all time, yet he would be the first to admit Shankly's influence ran through his team like a rich vein of gold. An incredible manager who somehow bettered even Shankly's record with a glorious period of trophies, titles and unsurpassed supremacy, despite this you'd have been hard pressed to find a more humble, good-natured man than Bob Paisley.

Paisley polished the diamonds coming through the Anfield youth system and spent wisely when he had to – Graeme Souness, Kenny Dalglish and Alan Hansen proved to be the backbone of the team during the mid-to-late seventies and were all signed by Paisley. A lovely guy with a wry sense of humour.

MANAGERIAL STATS

	PLD	W	D	L
League	378	212	99	67
FA Cup	36	20	7	9
League Cup	53	32	13	8
Europe	61	39	11	11
Other	6	4	1	1
Totals	**534**	**307**	**131**	**96**

TROPHIES

First Division x 6
League Cup x 3
FA Charity Shield x 6

European Cup x 3
UEFA Cup x 1
UEFA Super Cup x 1

There was only one Bob Paisley, and he was the greatest of them all. He went through the card in football. He played for Liverpool, he treated the players, he coached them, he managed them and then he became a director.

KENNY DALGLISH

There is no magic formula, there is no mystery about Anfield, it's just down to pure talent. Bob Paisley epitomises that and I am amazed that people in football, who ought to know better, do not accept the fact... The man oozes talent and he talks more common sense than ten of us managers put together and he probably works harder than ten of us put together as well!

BRIAN CLOUGH

I said that when I took over that I would settle for a drop of Bell's once a month, a big bottle at the end of the season and a ride round the city in an open top bus!

BOB PAISLEY

The secret is that our Liverpool team never know when to stop running and working. At Anfield we have always believed in players supporting each other and concentrating on not giving the ball away. You can't go charging forward all the time, willy-nilly. You must have patience, and this is where we can play the Continentals at their own game.

BOB PAISLEY

Kenny Dalglish
1985 – 1991 and 2011 – 2012

But for being banned in Europe during most of his reign as Liverpool boss, Dalglish could possibly have emulated even his old manager Bob Paisley. His six years as Anfield chief were the club's last real golden years of the modern era, and how high the Reds may have flown under the tenure of "King Kenny", one can only guess.

The only manager who could claim to have been a true Anfield great, Dalglish managed to make the transition from player to boss smoothly, but the tragic events of Hillsborough were ultimately too much to bear. His compassion to the bereaved families will always be remembered on Merseyside and, if anything, increased his standing even more among the Liverpool fans.

MANAGERIAL STATS

	PLD	W	D	L
League	280	160	69	51
FA Cup	45	28	12	5
League Cup	38	25	7	6
Europe	4	1	2	1
Other	14	9	4	1
Totals	**381**	**223**	**94**	**64**

TROPHIES

First Division x 3
FA Cup x 2
Charity Shield x 4

Kenny Dalglish knew his players. We never even had any set pieces really. He just went out and said: 'Go and beat them.' We never worked on patterns of play, which people would be amazed at now.

JOHN ALDRIDGE

Liverpool always outed at the first sign of decline. Then they'd give a new player a season or two to look at the scene before moving into the first team. I can tell you when I was a manager there, I never enjoyed such a luxury. Kenny came through Heysel and Hillsborough with some of his players. He'd become so emotionally involved with the whole Liverpool thing that he found it hard to say thanks, but no thanks.

GRAEME SOUNESS

If Liverpool had waited until the summer, and then asked me to go back as manager, I would have gone back.

KENNY DALGLISH

It has been an honour and a privilege to have had the chance to come back to Liverpool Football Club as manager.

KENNY DALGLISH

Rafa Benitez
2004 – 2010

Rafa Benitez could not hide his joy when he was announced as Liverpool manager and he would oversee Champions League success in his first season, with the famous "Miracle of Istanbul" as the Reds recovered from 3-0 down to beat AC Milan on penalties.

A popular manager with the fans and players alike, Benitez was a master tactician and had a great eye for players, bringing in the likes of Luis Garcia, Xabi Alonso and Fernando Torres, as well as improving the likes of Jamie Carragher into one of the best defenders in Europe. A largely enjoyable time for a manager who is fondly remembered at Anfield.

MANAGERIAL STATS

	PLD	W	D	L
League	228	126	55	47
FA Cup	17	9	3	5
League Cup	17	11	0	6
Europe	85	49	16	20
Other	3	2	0	1
Totals	**350**	**197**	**74**	**79**

TROPHIES

FA Cup x 1

FA Community Shield x 1

Champions League x 1

UEFA Super Cup x 1

Rafa Benitez reminds me of Shanks. He understands the game, how to get the best from individuals, how to change a game with substitutions and his tactics are sound. He has gradually built a squad that looks far stronger than last season, combining class, pace, excellent movement and strength in depth.

TOMMY SMITH

Even after five years with Rafa, I still feel I want to please him, that I want to impress him in every game I play. The great managers are like that. There are a handful operating on a different level and I am lucky enough to play for two of them, Benitez and Fabio Capello.

STEVEN GERRARD

"

We are preparing a special weightlifting plan for Gerrard's shoulders because we want him to lift a lot of trophies for Liverpool in the next few years! I am not in favour of selling him and we are building a great team around him because we want him to be the skipper who wins the most titles in Liverpool's history.

"

RAFA BENITEZ

"

It feels as if I have been on a permanent honeymoon since I arrived here. I am on a cloud and I feel as if with Liverpool I have found the love of my life.

"

RAFA BENITEZ

Jürgen Klopp

2015 – 2024

For many, if you had to embody the spirit and passion of Liverpool Football Club into flesh and blood, chances are you'd come out with something pretty close to Jürgen Klopp. For eight roller-coaster years, Klopp's "heavy metal" style of football, played by his "mentality monsters", thrilled not only Anfield, but the football world in general.

Klopp wore his heart on his sleeve and just *got* what LFC is all about, creating a bond with his players and the supporters that will be hard to replicate. But for a magnificent Manchester City side, Klopp may have left as the Reds' most successful manager – but to run Pep Guardiola's side so close so many times is testament to the fantastic era Klopp presided over.

MANAGERIAL STATS

	PLD	W	D	L
League	334	209	78	47
FA Cup	29	16	5	8
League Cup	32	21	2	9
Europe	91	56	14	21
Other	5	3	0	2
Total	**491**	**305**	**99**	**87**

TROPHIES

Premier League x 1

FA Cup x 1

League Cup x 2

FA Community Shield x 1

Champions League x 1

UEFA Super Cup x 1

FIFA Club World Cup x 1

I will miss him a lot. Jürgen played a really important part in my life: he brought me to another level as a manager. I think we respect each other incredibly. I just want to say thank you very much for the kind words but behind me, there are a lot of things that this club provided and give to me. Otherwise alone I cannot do it, I'm humble enough to understand completely that. He helped me many times with his team, a big competitor in my life.

PEP GUARDIOLA

I have to say, this comeback has one name – Jürgen. This is not about tactics, this is not about philosophy. This is about heart, soul and fantastic empathy that he's created with this group of players.

JOSÉ MOURINHO

"

I'm the normal one.

"

JÜRGEN KLOPP

"

There's hope and it's football. We are not in a situation where we say it will happen 100% but it's football. The character of the boys... two of the world's best strikers are not available and we have to score four goals to go through in 90 minutes. As long as we have 11 players on the pitch, we will try for 90 minutes to celebrate the Champions League campaign to give it a proper finish. That's the plan. If we can do it, wonderful. If we can't do it, let's fail in the most beautiful way.

"

JÜRGEN KLOPP

Appearance records
as of 31/01/2025

Most appearances in all competitions:
Ian Callaghan, 857

Most appearances as a goalkeeper:
Ray Clemence, 470

Most league appearances: **Ian Callaghan, 640**

Most FA Cup appearances: **Ian Callaghan, 79**

Most European appearances:
Jamie Carragher, 150

Most consecutive appearances: **Phil Neal, 417**
from 23 October 1976 to 24 September 1983

Youngest first-team player:
Jerome Sinclair, 16 years and 6 days
against West Bromwich Albion, 26 September 2012

Youngest player to reach 100 appearances:
Michael Owen, 19 years and 363 days

Oldest first-team player:
Ned Doig, 41 years and 165 days
against Newcastle United, 11 April 1908

Goal-scoring records

as of 31/01/2025

Record goal-scorer: **Ian Rush, 346**

Most goals in a season: **Ian Rush, 47**
in the 1983–84 season

Most league goals in a season:
Roger Hunt, 41
in the 1961–62 season

Most FA Cup goals: **Ian Rush, 39**

Most European goals: **Mohamed Salah, 50**

Fastest goal scored in a match:
Paul Walsh, 14 seconds
against West Ham United, 27 August 1984

Most hat-tricks: **Gordon Hodgson, 17**

Youngest goal-scorer:
Ben Woodburn, 17 years, 45 days
against Arsenal, 28 August 1994

Oldest goal-scorer:
Billy Liddel, 38 years, 55 days
against Arsenal, 28 August 1994

"

This is Anfield

"

The sign above the players' tunnel, installed by Bill Shankly, to remind the opposition they were not there for a good time and for his own players to remember who they were playing for.